Angels

A Sweet and Simple Introduction for Everyone

MAGGIE ANN ENGEL

Balboa Press books may be ordered through booksellers or by contacting:

Balboa Press
A Division of Hay House
1663 Liberty Drive
Bloomington, IN 47403
www.balboapress.com
844-682-1282

Interior Image Credit: Johnny Dame

ISBN: 978-1-9822-5995-2 (sc)
ISBN: 978-1-9822-5996-9 (e)

Library of Congress Control Number: 2021908760

Print information available on the last page.

Balboa Press rev. date: 04/27/2021

BALBOA.PRESS
A DIVISION OF HAY HOUSE

Contents

Introduction

As humans, we can have lots of feelings and fears that can be really uncomfortable for us and may be hard for us to manage at times. The magnificent and beautiful truth of it, though, is that there are benevolent and divine sources always there and available to support and help us but many of us don't know that!

We are in a time of great awakening across our Mother Earth, the angelic realm and guides of the light are here to help. Angels are beautiful, loving energies of the light. Their pure essence is one of complete and total unconditional love. Angels are here on Earth to help humans grow, learn, and deepen our understanding of our own divine nature.

We are all beings of God, created in likeness of the Divine. We have the ability to live a life full of love, joy, magic, safety, comfort, and peace. The angels are here to help us learn to do this.

The only thing is we have to ask! We have to reach out to the angels, through the divine order of the universe they are usually unable to help, except in extreme circumstances, unless we ask.

This book will introduce you to some of the Archangels more commonly known. It will teach you about their specific roles, and give you insight into your guardian angel's role as well.

The Archangels have their own specialties that they are particularly involved in and able to help with. The important thing to remember, though, is there is never any need to be specific, this is merely a guide. The angels will always help, whether you remember their name, their role or specialty, your intention in asking for help with anything is all that matters. For example, I have a special relationship with Archangel Ariel and I ask for her help with everything! The angels are wise and brilliant beyond our capacity to understand and all they ever want is to help you and love you! They will be able to guide the entire angelic realm to assist you when you ask!

This book also gives a description of their color, and the way their energy feels. The important thing for you to know is that this is my experience of each particular angel! You may experience each Archangel very differently and that is OK! The angels come to us in the exact way that is right for us in every moment.

When you spend time with the angels you will start to experience their energy and you will gain a feeling and a sense about each of them and develop a deeper relationship with those that are able to assist, guide, and love you best at any given time!

Archangel Gabriel

I am Archangel Gabriel, the divine messenger of God. Throughout time, I have carried so many messages of love, comfort, light, inspiration, creative genius, and vitally important information to people all over the world.

Sometimes I come in dreams with messages. During quiet time, I may show up with gentle inspiration. At times, my declarations are clearly heard, and other times, they come as brilliant ideas or thoughts. I show up in the best possible way for you!

I love to work with all forms of communication and creativity. If you are working on a project, writing a paper, or creating art, music, poetry, really any creation, you can call on me for help. I will be there to inspire you and help you find the brilliant ideas you need.

When you find yourself in a situation where the words aren't coming easily for you or you are having trouble understanding what someone is trying to tell or teach you, ask for my help, and I will be there to make things clearer.

I am great at calming an overactive mind too! If you find yourself anxious or unable to focus, just reach out to me, and I will help soothe your busy mind.

I love helping with events like plays, concerts, programs, speeches, choir performances, and debates. Music, art, writing, and poetry are some of my favorite things! I will help you in expressing the beauty of your own soul through your creations. We all have the graceful spark of divine creation in us, and I can help you access that spark in you so you can share it with the world.

I am divinely white and shimmery copper in color, and I carry my copper trumpet with me. I am associated with the element of water as I help thoughts, ideas, inspirations, and creations flow easily and freely. From the simplest forms of communication like text messages to beautiful works of art, call upon me, and I will assist you always!

Archangel Ariel

I am Archangel Ariel, the lioness of God. I am the divine protector of Earth. I work directly with Mother Earth to bring peace, beauty, joy, love, and pure glee to all of Earth's inhabitants, especially when out in nature.

I love bridging the gap between the animal kingdom and humans. I work as a guide in nature to help you have friendly, respectful, safe encounters with animals in their own domain.

If you find yourself in the woods, on the beach, in the desert, anywhere out in nature, you may encounter a wild animal. It may bring you such joy or possibly even fear. I want you to know I am there with you during those experiences. You can call upon me to help calm your mind and heart. I will mediate the experience, keep you safe, and guide you with the skills to move respectfully and carefully in the animal's space.

I love to support your adventures in the natural world. Just call on me when camping, hiking, rafting, or just playing outside, and I will help you have joyful, magical, and safe adventures!

Healing is one of my skills too. I work directly with my friend the healing angel, Archangel Raphael. We heal animals, people, ecosystems, and Earth herself. Call on us in times of physical or emotional stress or pain, and we can bring comfort, healing, and loving light whenever asked.

Another big job of mine is helping humans open up and accept all the good things in life! I help fill your heart with joy and bliss during special times! Vacations, fun experiences, gifts, holidays, happy times with friends and family, hugs, and love are a few of the places I work my magic!

I am white with shimmery, sparkly pink all around me. I am called the lioness of God because I help people find the courage to live fully from their hearts, in nature and in their lives. I work with all elements of Earth, and I am directly connected with Mother Earth herself. I love being of service to humans and am always here to help when asked!

Archangel Sandalphon

I am Archangel Sandalphon, the archangel of music, poetry, prayer, and spoken word. I help you strengthen your bond with the Holy Spirit, God universe. I act as a bridge to help you communicate more clearly with the divine. If you have an important message or prayer to give to God, call upon me, and I will assist in the guidance and delivery of that message and help make it clear. I also assist God universe in connecting directly with you. Sometimes I deliver messages from God through musical lyrics or spoken word you hear in passing. I also help line up those experiences where you are in the "right place at the right time" for magical, divinely aligned experiences to occur.

I use musical frequencies to help heal and uplift the frequency of humans so that it is easier to hear God and the angels, to connect with divine love and peace, and to fill your heart with joy. If you find yourself attracted to a certain music and notice that it fills your body and heart with good feelings, you can be assured I'm there assisting you in connecting with the Holy Spirit. If you are sad, worried, or stressed, call upon me, and I will guide you to the perfect song or musician to help heal your weary heart.

I also work directly with musicians and aspiring musicians. If you are learning to play an instrument, sing in a choir, or deliver a message in spoken word, ask for my help, and I will guide you on your path. I will also help when you are feeling called to create music and poetry. I will strengthen that divine bond so that you'll have access to the full creative force provided by God universe.

I am the tallest of angels and am a brilliant turquoise color with streaks of sparkly white rays. My energy is very earthy as I am grounded in this realm to assist humans with divine connection.

Archangel Metatron

I am Archangel Metatron, the angel of presence and life.

I am one of two angels who walked the Earth as a human before I ascended to the status of an archangel. My path on Earth was so closely weaved with that of the divine, God universe, that I was given the great honor of archangel status. I now serve humans in many ways and help you deepen your connection with the divine.

I use sacred geometry to help heal people. I have a special cube, a Merkaba cube, sometimes called Metatron's cube, that I rotate through your energetic body to help clear and cleanse your body of lower energies or feelings of unease. It is a gentle, simple process and requires only that you ask something like, "Metatron, please clear and cleanse my body and energy." Then relax, as my healing will uplift you, fill you with joy, and help you on all levels.

I especially love working with children and young people, as I myself am quite childlike. I love adventure, joy, and magical experiences. By connecting with me, you will be more fully present to step into your whole divine self. You will feel more confident, at ease, and graceful.

I am also great at math, and I'm an excellent record keeper and organizer. If you need assistance with any of these, call upon me, and I will be a great help.

I have a special relationship with children and young people who have labels like ADHD, ADD, autism, anxiety, and many more, those people whose brains work just a little differently than their peers. If you have one of these labels, I am a constant ally for you and can be of great service and comfort to you. I can help you realize your gifts and the beauty and uniqueness you are here to share. Ask for my help, and I will be there.

I am brilliant green and pink in color. I am here to help raise your energy to a more positive and loving state, and I am always so excited to help!

Archangel Michael

I am Archangel Michael, he who is like God.

I am one of the easiest archangels to connect with as I am ever present and work so closely with humans.

I am here to help you process through and release any and all uncomfortable emotions like fear, worry, doubt, anxiety, anger, guilt, shame, and disappointment. When you call upon me, I bring a brilliant, divine white light of love and peace, and I surround your entire being with it. This light draws out any negativity or lower energies into it and transforms those energies back to love.

I am especially helpful in the development of courage as well. If there is something you have been wanting to do or try that you are still mustering up the courage to, call upon me, and I will help give you the light and inner strength to follow your heart's desires.

I am particularly helpful with the emotion of fear. Where fear is present, it is blocking our connection to love and light. Some fear is appropriate when you are a human. For example, you may get scared when you see a large wild animal you are unfamiliar with. Fear is a natural response. In situations like that, ask for my assistance, and I will help guide the situation to a loving, safe conclusion and dissolve the fear.

The fear of things that you make up or imagine in your own mind that don't actually exist, that fear is unnecessary. As humans, many of you have brains that are wired to do that though. These baseless fears create so much stress for you, and I want to help you clear those fears from your mind, thoughts, emotions, and energy field. Please ask for my help whenever you are in a state of fear, real or imagined, and I will calm your head and heart and fill your space with love.

I am always here to protect you, keep you safe, and guide you toward your divine path in this life.

I am a brilliant white light of energy and sometimes appear with sparkly royal-blue streaks. I am large, gentle, warm, powerful, and loving. I emanate so much love and light that it is not unusual to feel my loving presence when you call upon me. I carry a beautiful white sword of light that I use to cut through any lower energy or negativity. I am delighted to be of service to you. Call upon me, and I will instantly be with you.

Archangel Raziel

I am Archangel Raziel, the keeper of the secrets and mysteries of the divine universe of God. I'm likened to a magician! I help you understand and connect with the magical qualities of the universe.

As humans, you are not born with a complete understanding of the divine universe and its unlimited potential. You are meant to grow, evolve, and deepen your understanding of the magical mysteries of it all throughout your lifetime.

I can help you in this process. I am here to assist you in connecting with the magic that lives in your heart that you are here on Earth to express! The key to this is joy. Joy is the conduit by which we gain access to our magic, uniqueness, and how we are here express it. Pay attention to those things that fill your heart with love and bring you joy. Call upon me, and I will help you cultivate those experiences that lift you and connect you with your own magic and joy!

I can also help you develop your intuition and insights in life. Oftentimes, my guidance comes as a beautiful, electric idea from out of nowhere. It can also be a subtle thought that grows into an idea that brings you wonderful experiences of joy, magical adventures, and fun!

I am here to guide you on a path of understanding and deepening your relationship with God universe and all the mysteries that exist here on Earth. I will guide you in ways that will deepen your understanding of yourself, as this will help in understanding the mysteries of all that is.

I am sparkly and rainbow-colored. My energy feels fun and electric. I work with all the elements of Earth to guide you on your path. I will be there to connect you with your joy, love, magical energy, and divine mission.

Archangel Chamuel

I am Archangel Chamuel, he who sees God. I am the divine angel of love, light, peace, compassion, and kindness.

I have been helping humans on Earth connect with the vibration of love and peace throughout all times. I even worked directly with Jesus and Buddha when they walked the Earth. You can be assured that I am working with spiritual leaders all over the world, as my main mission is global peace, love, and acceptance.

I can help you cultivate love, compassion, and acceptance for yourself. This is my number 1 way of guiding you on your path to long-lasting peace for yourself and the whole world. You are all truly unique and have beauty and light to shine forth to the world. I will guide you to connect to that light and beauty in yourself.

I am helpful at bringing in situations, people, and experiences that will provide you long-lasting peace. I do this by introducing you to the people, places, activities, and circumstances that are right for you and your unique vibrations.

I guide you to specific hobbies that help you quiet your mind and truly enjoy yourself.

I can help bring a special friend into your life that you feel peaceful, joyful, and loving with. I bring in the experiences that help you feel completely free and open to express and share your authentic self.

In times of anxiety, worry, tension, or just too much thinking, call upon me. I will help ease all those feelings and bring in peaceful love energy to calm your mind.

I am a beautiful, soft pink in color with bursts of sparkly white light throughout. I work to guide you to your most peaceful, loving life in every way that is perfect to the uniqueness of you!

Archangel Jophiel

I am Archangel Jophiel, the beauty of God. I help humans connect to the beauty and grace that resides within and throughout every bit of creation.

I can help you see the abundance of beauty that lives within you. I help you learn to really love and value yourself as the unique being you are. All humans are divine creations of God, and sometimes you become separated from that fact and forget the pure magnificence of you. It is vitally important for you to love and value yourself; it is the key to your greatest power and highest path in this life. Call upon me when you need help learning to fully and completely love and accept yourself. I want to help you see yourself as God sees you—beautiful and divine.

If you are seeking to create something of beauty for yourself or the world, I will be there to help. God's love and grace flow out through you when you create. I am here to support that process for you. Art and beauty come in infinite forms, with unlimited potential. As humans, the goal is to listen to your heart when creating. The beauty flows from there.

I can also help you gain clarity about what, how, and when you want to create. Even general clarity about yourself and what you love falls under my domain. If you find yourself seeking a deeper understanding of who you really are and what brings you joy, ask for my help, and I will bring clarity in your quest.

In the divine realms, we are not tied to the subjective judgment of beauty that humans often are. We see the divine beauty and magic in all of creation, in every being, and I can help you see that too!

I am a beautiful, sparkly, pale yellow with deep, sparkly magenta streaks throughout. I desire so deeply to open your eyes to the beauty, grace, and magic that is present everywhere in creation. Call on me, and I will help shift your perceptions.

Archangel Raguel

I am Archangel Raguel, a friend of God. I am a bright, joyous angel who works primarily to help human relationships of all kinds. I strive to bring peace, balance, and harmony to all relationships and situations.

I am particularly helpful if you are in a disagreement or argument with someone. You can call upon me to help bring a peaceful, fair conclusion to the discord.

As humans, it is totally natural and normal to have situations that bring disagreements, even with those whom you love the most. The goal of all discord is growth and learning. You have come to grow and expand your soul to be closer to the divine. I can help resolve situations peacefully and help you understand the greater lessons of these experiences. This will help you and those involved respond from a higher place of love and learning when discord occurs again.

I love guiding you to new relationships that are loving, supportive, and fun as well. If you are in need of new, like-minded, loving friends, call upon me, and I will have magical ways of helping you meet the right people at the right time.

I can also help create more love, fun, and harmony in your existing relationships. I enjoy guiding you in all the ways that help you build strong, supportive, and loving connections with others.

I am strongly aligned with fairness and justice too. I have been known to champion the underdog and am always in alignment with what is in the highest good for all. If you find yourself supporting a cause for social justice—like housing the homeless, feeding the hungry, or helping those in poverty—I will be there every step of the way. Just ask for my help!

I'm also a great advocate for our Mother Earth. I will help with any causes directed at benefiting the health, wellness, and sustainability of our Earth.

I am a radiant ice blue in color, and I bring a joyful, uplifting energy with me. I enjoy helping you with your relationships and social and environmental causes.

Archangel Uriel

I am Archangel Uriel, the light of God. I help with intelligence, brilliant ideas, understanding, forgiveness, and overall general wellness of your whole life. I bring light to everything!

If you find yourself having trouble with your homework or a particular subject at school, ask for my help! Sometimes my help comes as brilliant flashes of insight, which help you immediately understand the problem you were having. Other times, my help may come as subtle nudges, guiding you to the people or places that can help you understand the problem at hand.

I am also great with giving you insight and creative ideas when you are working on a project. If you are in a creative process for yourself or a project at school, call upon me, and I will give you those brilliant ideas that will help your project or creation flow beautifully out of you!

I love helping you learn and excel at school in all ways. Ask for my help when it is time to take a test or a quiz, and I will help you remember and access the answers and information that you have stored in your brain. I also like to guide you to the perfect study partners and groups that will help you with your academic growth.

When you find yourself in a misunderstanding of any kind, I love to help! I can help you understand the other person's point of view and help greatly with forgiveness, compassion, and understanding. The beautiful thing is, when you ask for my help, I also illuminate the misunderstanding for them and allow them the ability to understand where you're coming from, if they choose to! I love to help bring love, light, and healing to these situations!

I also assist with self-forgiveness. If you are feeling guilt or shame or you are upset at yourself over actions from the past, I can help you release those feelings into the light. The practice of self-forgiveness is very important for you as a human. Humanity can be messy at times; you may say or do hurtful things. It is truly important to love and forgive yourself through these moments though. You are here to learn and grow, and all these situations help you to do just that!

I am a beautiful golden color. My energy frequency is so high that you can often feel a warmth and sensation of love wash over when I am near. I am here to help you raise your frequency on all levels, intellectually, physically, emotionally, energetically, and spiritually.

Archangel Jeremiel

I am Archangel Jeremiel, the mercy of God. I work primarily to help you understand and heal your emotional world.

As humans, you tend to have very complex emotions and emotional responses. Sometimes you even have patterns of emotional responses that can be hard to understand. These patterns can be a response to a situation that is something you tend to repeat. For example, you may have a tendency to get mad at your mom because she doesn't let you do something you want to do. You may actually be mad because you fear missing out on something fun. So that fear/anger response may cause you to yell, then you get sent to your room. You calm down some, but the anger turns to sadness. Then the sadness turns to loneliness. You're left with this very complex emotional experience that doesn't feel good and is hard to understand. You may tend to repeat this same pattern over and over again. I can be of great help here! I can provide comfort and love during the experience and also help you understand how not getting what you wanted ended up with you being sad and lonely. The great thing is, I can help you heal these patterns with illumination, insight, awareness, understanding, and love!

Emotions aren't negative; they are tools and gifts you've been given to help you learn, grow, and move in the direction of your highest life.

Emotions aren't facts though; they are experiences to be understood and felt and allowed to flow freely through you.

I can help you have more of the feelings you enjoy like love, happiness, peace, hope, and joy. I do this by helping you understand and process through some of the more difficult emotions and emotional patterns.

My guidance is usually very subtle. I can come in dreams or in your thoughts. Sometimes repeating thoughts is me trying to get your attention.

I am a soft, deep, sparkly purple color. My energy is gentle and bright. I love helping you emotionally grow and mature in the direction of your highest and best life!

Archangel Zadkiel

I am Archangel Zadkiel, the keeper of the violet flame. I am here to assist you in times of worry, fear, stress, and discomfort. You can call upon me and ask that I help turn your uncomfortable feelings into more positive, loving ones.

I can help where there is conflict. If you are feeling resentful or angry toward a friend, sibling, parent, or anyone, you can call upon me, and I can help fill your heart with love, compassion, and forgiveness. I can heal hard and painful memories of the past and help fill your mind with love.

If you are feeling lost and anxious about your future, I can comfort you. I help you remember your true life's purpose here—a purpose of love and connection to the divine.

If you have lost an item, a favorite toy, book, object, ask for my help. I will guide you to where it is, with subtle, loving nudges. Sometimes it takes a bit, but I will help you find it!

I am also great at helping you remember things you forgot, like answers on a test or people's names! Just ask for my assistance, and I will provide.

I have a beautiful, mystical, healing flame I carry with me always. I use this to help burn through layers of falseness, illusion, heavy emotional experiences, and dense energies.

I'm violet in color and carry my healing violet flame with me. I love helping with mercy, love, compassion, memory, forgiveness, and truth. Call on me anytime. Simply ask for my help, and I will be there.

Archangel Raphael

I am Archangel Raphael, the healer of God. My main mission is one of healing on all levels. I help heal emotional, physical, mental, energetic, and spiritual blocks and wounds of all kinds. I am also helpful at healing things that aren't specifically human too. I help heal animals, plants, places, relationships, ideas, structures, thought patterns, belief systems, patterned emotional responses, and injustices. You name it, I can help heal it!

If you, a loved one, or a friend is ever suffering from illness of any kind, call on me. I will use my healing energies to ease any discomfort, and my light will bring love and peace to all in need. All that is ever needed is for you to ask for my help.

There are many times when people suffer and experience pain and heartache for themselves or others. I am always available to help in these situations. One does not have to have an illness to ask for my help. I help heal all wounds, even those that don't appear as wounds but instead hurt our hearts or cause internal discomfort or emotional unease. My healing transcends all levels. Anytime you are feeling unwell in any way or you or someone or something is suffering, call upon me. My loving energy will help bring everything back to the heart, to love, balance, and peace.

I so greatly wish to help heal the planet on all levels as well. Mother Earth is such a unique and beautiful place of learning, growth, and love. I call on you to ask for my help in healing Mother Earth every day. The more people ask, the more I am able to help. Together we can bring this special planet back to an optimal state of health.

I am a beautiful, deep green color with streaks of sparkly gold throughout. My energy is soothing, comforting, and full of love. I want nothing more than to be of service to all the inhabitants of Mother Earth and to help restore everything there to a place of love, health, peace, and balance.

Archangel Azrael

I am Archangel Azrael, he whom God helps. My role as an archangel is a very powerful, tender, loving, and sweet one. I am the gatekeeper between realms. I am with you as you transition into this world through birth and as you leave this realm through death.

I help your mother and your soul prepare for the process of you entering into a new life in a human body. I provide calm, soothing reassurance, and love to you as a sweet little baby. You are wrapped in a gentle, soothing white light as you transition from the heavenly realms to the earthly plane. The love, calm, and peace you and your mother feel in this process is me gently guiding you in.

Throughout your life, I am present with you. I am quiet, in the background. I am not an angel who interacts much with humans on the earthly plane of existence. While you are growing, learning, evolving, living, and aging, I am a loving, familiar presence, observing and providing an air of peace and comfort.

When the time comes for a soul to transition back to the heavenly realms, my presence is familiar, peaceful, and safe, as I have been providing love all along. I am there at every human's transition. My role in that process is gentle and full of love and light. No matter what the circumstances of a person's passing, I ensure peace and love are felt so as to make the transition gentle and easy.

I am present with grieving loved ones as well. I help bring grace, comfort, and a certain amount of lightness in the times surrounding a person's passing. My presence helps loved ones access the joyful and happy memories of their shared life together, to celebrate the magnificence of their loved one's existence, to feel all this love, along with the grief.

Unlike the other angels, it is not necessary to ask for my help. My role is ordained and set. I help all souls that come to Earth as humans in the transitions of birth and death. I am always available to make you more aware of my presence and love though. You can call upon me, and I will bring comfort, love, and peace.

My energy is calm, quiet, loving, gentle, and soft. I appear in a way that is most soothing to the souls I am assisting, sometimes colorful, sometimes soft, creamy, light, and white. My role is one of utmost importance, and you can be assured that my love and grace are strongly felt by all those on a journey of transition.

Guardian Angel

It is I, your Guardian Angel. I have known you from before you were born. I have been with you every moment you have been in your body.

I am a constant source of love, support, and complete and total acceptance. I see you truly as you are and I love you for it. You are a totally unique human being. There has never been and will never be anyone like you and I'm such a lucky angel to be your guardian.

I help you with everything as I am always with you. I like to communicate with you in ways you can feel and sense, subtle and often. It is best to stay in a peaceful, calm, easy way to connect with my communications. If you are having trouble maintaining peaceful energy, ask for my assistance, I will be right there with a wave of peace to help you a long.

I can help you to feel the emotions that are keeping you from being in a calm, easy way, be present with them, let the emotions pass through, and return to an easy state.

I love being your Guardian angel and couldn't imagine a greater mission in the world. My main job is to love and protect you. I also work to guide you on or to your highest path for this lifetime.

My color varies depending on you and where you are in your lifetime and the energies you are most present with. To connect with me and feel the tremendous love I have for you, find a quiet spot, close your eyes, and focus all of your attention to center of your chest, your heart center. Consciously feel the sensations there, relax the energy, if needed, and allow the sensations of love and light to fill your heart space. My love is always present there for you to feel and experience. I have pure divine love for you, my human.

Printed in the United States
by Baker & Taylor Publisher Services